BELIEVING GOD

A TRUE STORY OF
DAY-BY-DAY HEALING
AND RESTORATION

*"FOR WE WALK BY FAITH
AND NOT BY SIGHT"*

2 CORINTHIANS 5:7

MARILYN MARINELLI

Table of Contents

About the Author

Marilyn Marinelli

Marilyn Marinelli is an Ordained Minister of the gospel of Jesus Christ, associated with Faith Christian Fellowship Int'l, a worldwide full gospel fellowship. She is also the Co-Founder of The Fellowship of Christian Poets, a worldwide ministry, and Co-Author of "Together Forever" a marital enrichment home seminar.

She ministered for the Fellowship of Christian Poets for over 10 years through a monthly article called "Ministry for the Poets Soul". She has ministered in song at various churches.

She is also the Founder and President of Have A Heart

for Companion Animals, Inc. a ministry dedicated to the protection of companion animals. www.haveaheart.us She also is co producer and singer of "The Johnny Mello Show" a group of 6 singers that do fundraising events to raise money for her non-profit organization.

She is the author of another Christian book titled "A Dry And Thirsty Land" which is a book that ministers to women sharing true victories in her walk with the Lord.

All the glory goes to God for His grace that He has shared with her and is still sharing in times of need.

One of her deepest desires is to share her knowledge of God, with others that have lost hope. Her greatest joy is to know that people are being set free from bondage by standing on the Word of God because of her ministry.

She is inspired by the Holy Ghost, and receives revelations from God in many situations. She hopes to shed light on sharing God's direction given to her with others so that His Words will speak to their hearts as it has hers, thereby, setting them free.

Marilyn's books are available for review and purchase at www.christianliferesourcecenter.org.

Introduction

I share my testimony of healing with you to encourage you in your walk with the Lord in any situation you may be facing. "Faith Is The Substance Of Things Hoped For, The Evidence of Things Not Seen." Hebrews 11:1

I encourage you to take Faith as your substance to overcome your circumstance. The secret is in what you believe.

This is a diary I kept as I walked through towards my healing from an accident caused by a chiropractor. I had no doctor except the one that had caused my injury to help me, so I started to trust in the Lord for my direction and healing. I waited almost a month until I was able to see a new chiropractor that was a, "Born Again", Christian. The Lord led me to him.

Come with me on this journey to healing and be blessed and encouraged in your walk with God. We will touch the hem of Jesus' garment together by faith.

It has been 18 years later now and God has kept every promise to me.

This is scripture of faith that I said and
stood on for many months.

"And, behold, a woman... came behind Him, and touched
the hem of His garment; for she said within herself,
If I may but touch His garment, I shall be whole."

--Matthew 9:20-21

CHAPTER 1

PIPELINE TO JESUS

MAY 1995

A FEW MONTHS BEFORE THIS INJURY happened I was living in Wisconsin. My husband and I hadn't moved back to Florida, as yet. I had attended a worship service at "Pipeline to Jesus". Just before we left the service an older gentlemen came up to me and handed me a dollar bill. He said, "This dollar bill has all seven's on it which represents perfection". He said to me "you will be receiving a miracle". He than touched my head and mentioned Psalm 91 to me. I went back and fell flat on my back. I remembered how interesting that this man mentioned Psalm 91. I had been reading this psalm and encouraging myself through it and even sent a letter to someone I didn't know in the military for encouragement. It struck me so funny to think that this man would mention Psalms 91 to me. God had been showing me Psalms 91 and I was trying to memorize the whole Psalm. It starts out with "He that **dwells (stays)** in the secret place of the most high shall abide under the shadow of the Almighty (under his protection) and I will say of the Lord he is **my strength** and **my refuge in him will I trust**." Little did I know that I would really be going through something in the near future and that I was to stay under the protection of God and that he would be my strength and my refuge and I would really trust in Him. Going back to what took place that night. Laughter enveloped me as I lay on the floor. I just kept laughing and laughing with joy. This may seem odd to you but that is what happened. God sent this man to let me know that He was in control and would be there for me and that I would receive a miracle.

A few months past and my husband and I moved to back to Florida. There I was doing fine until I unpacked a number of items from our move and pulled a muscle or something on my side or my back I wasn't sure. Since, I had gone to chiropractors before, I wasn't in any fear of them, and so I made an appointment with a local chiropractor. This is where my story begins.

I went to a local chiropractor. He had a nice office and lots of clients. I went through an exam and x-ray. After receiving a number of adjustments from the chiropractor, while I was shopping in a small store, all of a sudden I looked up and the walls seemed to have moved right in front of my face. My vision was off. I new I didn't need glasses since I had just gone for an eye check up. What was happening? I thought. I had another appointment with the chiropractor and another adjustment. The following is what took place.

I went back to the same chiropractor. He said that my first vertebrae was out of place and that is why my vision was off and he proceeded to try to adjust me and put my bone back in alignment. My husband was with me but then left for work and was to come back at 12 noon. I was told by the chiropractor to go into another room and rest. Then he told some lady that worked for him to use some kind of massager on my neck and shoulder and upper back area all on the left side. He then came back and did something to my neck and told me to go into yet other room and just rest a while. Well, I picked up a magazine (there were other people around but they never noticed me.) As I was reading the magazine all of a sudden I slumped on to the couch and just laid there not being able to move at all. I could, however, just move my eyes around but nothing else. My husband felt led of the Lord to leave his work early…that he was suppose to check on me and it was a good thing he did. He arrived at the doctor's office and led back to where I was. When he saw me and noticed that I couldn't move or respond to him, he called out, "What did you do to my wife?" They called the doctor immediately and he and my husband took me back to a room and the doctor twisted my head and I was able to feel and move again. The doctor had me come back to his office on the following Saturday morning; to check me out and make sure I was alright. While waiting for him to arrive a gentlemen that did massages at his office, walked in the office and asked why I was there and as he placed his hand on my back he said, "Oh my, this bone is out of place". Just at that time the doctor arrived. He took my husband and I into an exam room and checked me to see if I had experienced a stroke. He said that I was alright. But I wasn't. Yeah thanks a lot, I think now.

My Injury

My neck, shoulder, and left back muscles were all jammed up and I couldn't raise my arm to get anything off even a lower shelve. My first vertebra was out of joint (which thank God the chiropractor fixed or I wouldn't have been able to move). A vertebra in the middle of my back that was resting on a nerve was damaging the nerve. I lost feeling in my left hand and was dropping things to the floor. I also lost sight to see strongly in my left eye. The blood flow to my head on my left side was being hampered so I would feel numbness in my head on that same side, I had to sleep with my arm above my head because it hurt my back too much to keep it at my side My strength, needless to say, was not available to me.

The vertebra in the middle of my back was resting on a nerve and was never addressed by the chiropractor. This was the key to my healing that only God took care of. You will learn how this all came about as you read on.

CHAPTER 2

MY VERY SPECIAL PSALM

Before I go on with my story, I would like to share with you my very special Psalm. Psalm 27 is my cry to God, always.

PSALM 27

"The Lord is <u>my light</u> and <u>my salvation</u>; whom shall I fear? The Lord is the <u>strength </u>of my life; of whom shall I be afraid? When the wicked, even mine enemies and my foes, came upon me to eat up my flesh, <u>they stumbled and fell</u>. Though a host should encamp against me, my heart shall not fear; though war should rise against me, in this will I be confident. One thing have I desired of the Lord, that will I seek after; that I may dwell in the house of the Lord all the days of my life, to behold the beauty of the Lord, and to inquire in his temple. For <u>in the time of trouble he</u> shall hide me; he shall set me up upon a rock. And now shall mine head be lifted up above mine enemies round about me: therefore will I offer in his tabernacle sacrifices of joy; <u>I will sing, yes, I will sing praises unto the Lord.</u> Hear, O Lord, when I cry with my voice: have mercy also upon me, and answer me. When thou saidst, <u>seek ye my face</u>; my heart said unto thee, <u>Thy face, Lord will I seek.</u> Hide not thy face far from me; put not thy servant away in anger: thou hast been my help; leave me not, neither forsake me, O God of my salvation. When my father and my mother forsake me, then the Lord will take me up. Teach me they way, O Lord, and lead me in a plain path, because of mine enemies. Deliver me not over unto the will of mine enemies; for false witnesses are risen up against me, and such as breathe out cruelty. <u>I had fainted, unless I had believed to see the goodness of the Lord in the land of the living. Wait on the Lord: be of good courage, and he shall strengthen thine heart: wait, I say, on the Lord.</u>"

CHAPTER 3

WHAT WAS I GOING TO DO?

So here I was. What was I going to do? I cried unto the Lord and He directed me to a Christian Yellow Page booklet where I found a listing for a Christian chiropractor. I believed I was supposed to contact him. Guess what the new chiropractor's name was? Dr. Popwell. Isn't that something? How could I have missed the leading of the Lord? As it always seems to be when you call a doctor he was on vacation. But, he would be back soon. I had to wait From May 25th – June 9, 1995.

O.K God, now what do I do? I was filled with fear that I was going to die. I feared that I wouldn't ever be the same again and that the new doctor would take the side of the one that lied to me. I was angry. I felt I couldn't get well quick enough. I felt I was letting my husband down and that I was a burden. I wanted to drive and go to the store myself; I found it hard to sleep because of fear of the unknown. I was feeling isolated and alone, that my first vertebra would move and my head would not be sitting correctly where it needed to be and that my perception would go off and I would fall over again and not be able to move like in the doctor's office.

The following is an account of what happened between God and me while I was waiting for my appointment with Dr. Popwell.

MAY 25TH, 1995

God reminded me of this particular part of Psalms 23, "The Lord is my shepherd…I shall not want…He maketh me to lie down in green pastures…He leadeth me beside the still waters and restores my soul." This was the beginning of my restoration. Soul means mind, will and emotions. I lived by a quite stream (still waters), a patch of green grass off from my patio (green pasture) I understood what God was showing me. That it was He who was there for me and in the process would work on restoring me to good health, both physically and emotionally.

After prayer this morning and listing things I wanted to do, God gave me these words:

"Be it according to your Faith all these things shall be yours for you are bought with a price singularly suited to do my good works. To sing praises to my name, to enhance that which I direct your hands to do and be cheery in all well-being. **DO NOT** hesitate, **DO NOT** fear, for your redemption draweth near you. It is not the past to hope for. It is the present light that I shine upon you for you are bought with a price far better than rubies or gold. I have redeemed you from the curse. You are set free by me to do good works, to glorify me, to bring good tidings to the meek and humble for they need help, encouragement and trust.

For what shall I do for you? What ministry are you suited for? I have given you wealth in your heart, wisdom in your mind and an unblemished spirit, far better than rubies, for I am for you…to till and mold you to my likeness.

You cannot sit in darkness. Shine bright with your John (my husband) love him, embrace him, bring peace to him in love and deed.

DO NOT wander to do, but <u>rest in me.</u> I will enhance your way. <u>I will</u> do unto you what is best, for I am not against you but for you. For you are my shepherd girl who will see many saved. Stand firm in the midst of this darkness and let the light of life shine upon you, for I am <u>come to bring forth peace and strength</u> to your being.

DO NOT stir the water of doubt and fear. Let me rest beneath you and come stand upon my rock for there I will be."

These are the following scriptures God gave to me this day:

When I pray specifically for something and God reveals Himself in scripture to me, I read the scripture as if it was specifically spoken to me.

Exodus 4:5 "And the people (me) BELIEVED: and when they (I) heard that the Lord had visited the children of Israel (me that God visited) and that he had looked upon their (my) affliction (trouble), then they (I) bowed their (my) heads and worshipped (thanked God)."

To further show me that God was really talking to me, He lead me to **Psalms 113:9** "He maketh the barren (childless) woman to keep house and to be a joyful mother of children, Praise ye the Lord."

I am a childless woman who raised two stepchildren by God's direction. God was confirming through this scripture that He was speaking to me.

God's promise to me that day was:

Psalms 29:11 "The **Lord Will** give **strength** unto his people; (me) the Lord will bless his people (me) with peace."

Though I didn't see or feel my outward healing, that day I knew God was working in my life.

Chapter 4

My Special Time With God

Between May 25th And May 30th

My special times with the Lord concerning my healing as I waited for my first appointment with a new chiropractor, Dr. Popwell, which would be on June 9th.

The first thing God showed me as I walked out on to my back patio to look at the lake and passing ducks and talking to God was a palm tree. "Look at the tree", I heard him speak to my spirit. "Look at the tree, is not the trunk bent in various ways? See how it flourishes. Is it not healthy? If someone comes along and bends a part a different way everything else in the tree would be out of alignment since it's grown this way and been strong all these years. Only if I bend the whole tree and make it straight would it flourish. If not, it should be left alone to be the tree it is and it will flourish and be a good tree."

God was certainly showing me through the chiropractor I went to, who originally had injured me, that trying to make me straighter as he believed a person should was wrong. God, on the other hand, was showing me that if I had grown a certain way, I should be left alone. He was not telling me that I shouldn't be healed from my injury but that what was done to me should have been left alone. What this chiropractor did was put me out of alignment from how I had grown up normally.

As the days past, I still laid around with pain and bruises but, God was still talking to me as I watched a Christian television program. This is what he revealed to me, that I should do:

Confess healing and set the stage to my healing

Take the <u>WORD</u> **like** <u>MEDICINE</u>

God's <u>WORD is health to my body.</u>

God gave me the following scriptures:

Proverbs 4:20-27 "My son (or daughter) <u>attend to my words</u>; incline (your) thine ear unto my sayings. Let them <u>not depart</u> from (your) thine eyes; keep them in the midst of (your) thine heart. For <u>they are life</u> to those that find them, and <u>health to all their flesh</u>."

PSALMS 34

"I will bless the Lord at all times: his praise shall continually be in my mouth. My soul shall make her boast in the Lord: the humble shall hear thereof, and be glad. O magnify the Lord with me and let us exalt his name together. I sought the Lord, and he heard me, and delivered me from all my fear. They looked unto him, and were lightened: and their faces were not ashamed. This poor man (woman) cried, and the Lord heard him, (her) and saved him (her) out of all his troubles.

The angel of the Lord encampeth round about them that fear him, and delivereth them. O taste and see that the Lord is good: blessed is the man that trusteth in him. O fear the Lord, ye his saints: for there is no want to them that fear him. The young loins do lack, and suffer hunger, but <u>they that see the Lord shall not want for any good thing.</u>

Come, ye children, hearken unto me: I will teach you the fear of the Lord. What man is he (woman) that desireth life, and loveth many days, that he may see good? **Keep thy tongue, from evil, and they lips from speaking guile. Depart from evil, and do good: seek peace, and pursue**

it. The eyes of the Lord are upon the righteous, and his ears are open unto their cry. The face of the Lord is against them that do evil, to cut off the remembrance of them from the earth.

The righteous cry, and the Lord hearteth, and delivereth them out of all their troubles. The Lord is nigh (near) unto them that are of a broken heart, and saveth such as be of a contrite (crushed) spirit. Many are the afflictions of the righteous; but the Lord delivereth him out of them all. He keepeth all his bones: not one of them is broken. Evil shall slay the wicked and they that hate the righteous shall be desolate. **The Lord redeemeth the soul of his servants; and none of them that trust in him shall be desolate."**

The above scriptures gave me specific direction on what to do and how God was going to help me through my dilemma. I am to:

1. Pay attention and listen to God's words for me.

2. Keep God's words ever before me.

3. Keep Gods' words in my heart.

4. That God's words are health to my flesh.

5. Praise God all the time.

6. That I should seek God and He will hear me and deliver me out of my trouble.

7. That angels are around me and will deliver me.

8. Trust in God

9. Seek God and I shall not want for any good thing.

10. Do not speak evil or do evil but do good.

11. Look for peace and rest in it.

12. God will be with me.

13. God hears the cry of his children and delivers them from trouble.

14. God is near to the broken hearted and saves ones that have a crushed spirit.

My heartfelt response to the Lord was reflected in Psalms 119:57-62:

1. I would acknowledge God as all in all.

2. I would keep His words as truth.

3. Asked for His Mercy

4. Thought of my ways (attitudes).

5. Turned my thoughts and trust to God quickly.

6. Not to forget God's laws.

7. And to rise up in the night, and give Him thanks for my healing, care, mercy and love.

AND THE DAYS ROLL ON

God uses His people to minister to us. During this day I heard Dr. Cherry on Trinity Broadcasting and a lady from a local Jacksonville broadcast from Trinity both helping me in my FAITH walk with God. God even had a young woman sing three of my favorite songs that I have shared and performed at our own church and other places to minister to others. How good He is. This lady sang and ministered back to me "He Touched Me", "He'll Do It Again", and "Holy Ground". How blessed I was to think God would bless and minister to me this way.

I was rising in the mornings with fear and pain and yet I was rising and thanking God for my healing. Not only physically but also for healing emotional hurts.

TODAY IS MAY 30, 1995

My time with God today…

Hebrews 11:1 starts with "**Now** <u>faith is the substance of things hoped for, the evidence</u> **of things** <u>not yet seen</u>."

I encourage you to read the whole chapter about how many people received victory in their life because they held on to and used Faith in God's words that were spoken to them.

Faith is the Substance from which
God created miracles.

Next I read: **Psalms 119:73A** "Thy hands
have made me and fashioned me."

Psalms 119:76, 77, 78 "Let, I pray thee, thy merciful
kindness be for my comfort, according to thy word unto
thy servant (me). Let thy tender mercies come unto me,
that I may live: for thy law is my delight. Let the proud be
ashamed for they dealt perversely with me without cause:
but **I WILL mediate in they precepts (word)."**

**God reminds me that He made me (fashioned me) like
the tree he showed me in my back yard. I asked God to
show mercy to me. A proud physician injured me and
yet God showed me I should stay in His Word.**

CHAPTER 5

I GAVE MY INFIRMITIES TO JESUS

MAY 31ST, 1995

This morning I prayed and gave my infirmities to Jesus as the scriptures teach "Come unto me all that are heavy laden". **Isaiah 53:4 & 5** "Surely he hath borne our **Grief's**, and carried our Sorrows: yet we did esteem him stricken, smitten of God, and afflicted.

But he was wounded for **Our Transgressions**, he was bruised for Our Iniquities: the chastisement of **Our Peace** was upon Him: and **With His Stripes We Are Healed**."

God was saying to take the sickness and pain and lay it upon Jesus and walk away with my healing.

I put my hands on the places where my infirmities were and lifted them up to JESUS on the cross. I left my infirmities there and received my healing by FAITH.

The rest of the scriptures I received from the Lord this day were:

Matthew 9:22 "Daughter be of good COMFORT **THY FAITH** hath made thee (me) whole."

I have to say here that God gave this scripture to me over and over, no matter what version of the bible I looked at. He kept His word in front of my eyes through many days. So I wrote the scripture out on 4 pieces of paper and put them around my house so my eyes would look upon the promise God gave me. Plus **II Corinthians 10:5** "Casting down imaginations and every high thing that exalts itself against the knowledge of God." This scripture helped me to remember not to only accept God's promise but to attack the fears or pain that was going against what God was showing me each day.

The rest of the scriptures I received from the Lord that day were:

Luke 5:20 "And when he (Jesus) saw their (my) FAITH he said unto him, man (Marilyn) thy sins are forgiven thee."

Suddenly I realized that God was doing a deeper healing than just physical. He was actually restoring my soul (mind, will, and emotions) by helping me to identify unconfessed sin and cleansing me from them.

John 5:14 "Behold, (look) thou art made (healed) whole sin no more, lest a worse thing come unto thee."

Isaiah 40:31 "But they (me) that **wait** upon the Lord shall **renew** (be refreshed) their **strength** they **shall** mount up with wings as eagles; **they shall** run and **not be weary and they shall walk and not faint.**"

God told me today to use my praise and worship tapes and to praise and worship Him for 5 days (sing and dance).

I had pain but I trusted God – so I proceeded to Praise and Worship Him at home and when I went to church.

Little did I know, at that time, that God was having me do this to loosen myself up from the pain that I was having and so I would be exercising my muscles.

Here are the rest of the scriptures the Lord gave me this day.

Zechariah 10:12 "And **I WILL STRENGTHEN** them (me) **IN THE LORD**, and they (me) **shall** walk up and down in **his name**, saith the Lord."

Psalms 121 "**I Will** lift up mine (my) eyes unto the hill, from whence cometh my help. My help **cometh** from the Lord, which made heaven and earth. He will not suffer thy foot to be moved: **he will keepeth thee will not slumber (sleep).** Behold, **he that keepeth Israel neither slumber nor sleep. The Lord is thy keeper:** the Lord is thy shade upon thy right hand. The sun shall not smite thee by day, nor the moon by night. **The Lord shall preserve thy go-ing out and thy coming in from this time forth, and even for evermore.**"

Mark 11:22b & 23 "Have **FAITH** in God." For verily I say unto you, That whosoever (me) **shall say** unto this mountain. **BE THOU REMOVED** and **BE THOU CAST INTO THE SEA and SHALL NOT DOUBT IN HIS HEART,** BUT **SHALL BELIEVE THAT THOSE THINGS WHICH HE SAITH SHALL COME TO PASS,** he shall have whatsoever he saith."

I immediately started to stand against the mountain of pain and fear, commanding it to be removed from my presence and to be cast into the sea… in the name of JESUS. I had the confidence to do this because I was standing in FAITH, believing that what God had been saying in the scriptures to me would come to pass.

CHAPTER 6

MY TIME WITH THE LORD.

JUNE 1, 1995 – JUNE 6, 1995

JUNE 1, 1995

From this day on, I started to put walking tapes on, **every day**, and then graduated to an exercise tape (doing only what I could do).

Zechariah 10:12 "And **I will** strengthen them in the Lord; and they **shall** walk up and down in his name, saith the Lord."

God's promise to me was that He would remove oppression from me and restore me.

"For We Walk By Faith (Not By Sight)" II Corinthians 5:7

This is what the Lord spoke to my heart today and showed me what was to come:

"I **will** supply **all your needs.**"

"I **will** uphold you with the right hand of righteousness"

"I **will** heal thy land"

"I **will** bless my people"

"Sadness shall flee, darkness **shall move**, clouds **shall** cease, My light shall shine in the midst of thee for **I AM THAT I AM**. Seek Me, find Me, knock and the door shall be open the light of life shall shine forth as the noonday sun and I shall be a Father unto you with great mercy. Grace and wisdom shall be upon thy lips. Knowledge shall be in thy heart. **I WILL** not leave you comfortless, unable to move, but **WILL DELIVER** you and set you upon My wall. Praise My name, make mention of My cause for Jesus My Son **shall** visit you and shine peace in your heart, **DO NOT FEAR** or tremble for you are bought with a price, I am for you. You are My child. Strength and wisdom are yours, blessings will overtake you and you will mention My name to many."

Thank You God.

Big reminder! I am still waiting to see Dr. Popwell…. Let's continue:

June 2, 1995

I am still in pain, dancing and praising the Lord and still in the process of working towards my healing. I am still exercising and still sleeping in the afternoons.

My scriptures for today:

Psalms 103 "Bless the Lord, O my soul; and all that is within me, bless his holy name. Bless the Lord, O my soul, and **forget not all his benefits: who forgiveth all** (acceptance) thine iniquities; who **healtheth all** thy diseases; (health) who **redeemeth** (deliverance) **thy life from destruction**: who **crowneth thee with** (authority) **the with lovingkindness and tender mercies;** who **satisfieth** (provisions) **thy mouth** with good things; so that thy youth is renewed like the eagle's

The Lord executeth **righteousness and judgment** for all that are oppressed. He **made know his ways** unto Moses, his acts unto the children of Israel (revelation). The Lord is **merciful** and gracious slow to anger and plenteous in mercy. He will not always chide: neither will he keep his anger forever. He hath not dealt with us after our sins: nor rewarded us according to our iniquities (compassion). For as the heaven is high above the earth, so great is his mercy toward them that fear him. As far as the east is from the west so far hath he removed our transgressions from us. Like a father pitieth his children, so the Lord pitieth them that fear him. For he knoweth our frame: he remembereth that we are dust. As for man, his days are as grass: as a flower of the field, so he flourisheth. For the wind passeth over it, and it is gone: and the place thereof shall know it no more. But the mercy of the Lord is from everlasting to everlasting upon them that fear him, and his righteousness unto children's children; To such as keep his covenant, and to those that remember his commandments to do them. The Lord hath prepared his throne in the heavens; and his kingdom ruleth over all. Bless the Lord, ye his angels unto the voice of his word. Bless ye the Lord, all ye his hosts: ye ministers of his that do his pleasure. Bless the Lord, all his works in all places of his dominion: bless the Lord, O my soul." **(Psalms 103)**

This is what God spoke to my heart today:

"For I have not given you a spirit of fear (the spirit of fear that is upon me is not from God.) but a Spirit of power, of love and a sound mind. Go preach My word to the lonely, lost and confused. Set up a camp round about them. Fear Me and come forth from them all. For all have sinned and come short of the glory of God. Nothing is done without My spirit. Worship Me! Praise Me!, for I am worthy of your praise. Worship a new, for I have called you out of darkness into light. Do not hinder the baptism of My Holy Spirit for He will **be to you a covering of a great magnitude.** Many shall rejoice in Me, many shall be made whole, many shall see Me....for: **Psalms 104:5** "Who had laid the foundations of the earth that it should not be removed forever?"

God reminds me again:

Mark 5:34 "Daughter **THY FAITH** hath made thee whole go in peace and be whole of thy plaque."

Ezekiel 37: 5 "thus saith the Lord god unto these bones, behold, I will cause breath to enter into you and ye shall live and I will lay sinews (muscle) upon you and will bring flesh upon you and cover you with skin and put breath in you and ye shall live and ye shall know that I am the Lord."

From this scripture God showed me today that He was in control of my bones and muscles and that He will heal me.

Then God told me to read. When I asked where? He said read the Bible from the beginning....

So I added to my exercise, Praise and Worship time, prayer time to start to read from the beginning of the bible from that time on. What slowly became clear and got down in my heart was that God is in control of **everything**. Therefore, He is also in control of my situation.

What blessings and promises and teaching I have received today by sitting at the Lord's feet.

June 5, 1995

God gave me more scripture (promises). I am still hurting, tired, and getting better.

I have been praying for healing and family restoration and have kept God's Word in front of my eyes and listened to many pastors ministering…building my FAITH in God. **Romans 10:17** "FAITH comes by hearing and hearing by the word of God."

When I started this journey, I said, "Jesus? You said if I had FAITH as a grain of mustard seed I could speak to the mountain and it would be removed. Jesus? Take the little bit of FAITH I have and use it for my healing."

God Has Been Restoring My Walk, My Soul, and My Health

My scriptures for today are:

Isaiah 40:29 "He giveth power to the faint and to them that have no might be increaseth strength."

Jeremiah 30:29 "For **I Will Restore Health** unto thee and **I Will Heal Thee** of thy wounds saith the Lord."

June 6, 1995…Left side of my top part of my back (I call it my wing area) still feeling real bad. Still can't see well, still can't hold anything in my left hand, still very tired, still feel the pain in my back.

God's promise to me this morning:

Job 11: 16 & 17 "Because thou shall forget thy misery and remember it as waters that pass away, and thine age shall be clearer than the noonday, thou shalt shine forth thou shalt be as the morning."

God promised me that I would forget the misery I was going through and that I will feel young again refreshed.

During my Praise and Worship time today my back pain lifted.

Come out of fear and walk by faith….I was in a tremendous amount of fear from my accident.

My husband has been lifting me up in prayer everyday. Today he prayed for me against this spirit of fear before he left to go back to work from his lunch hour. I put TBN on and God is so good. There was a lady praying against fear …she was **saying fear cannot exist where FAITH is** and I prayed along with her and her husband against the spirit of fear. **The fear lifted from me.**

Proverbs 17:22

"A Merry Heart Doeth Good Like A Medicine"

I Samuel 2:10 "The adversaries of the Lord shall be broken to pieces: out of heaven shall be thunder upon them: the Lord shall judge the ends of the earth: and he shall give **strength** unto his king and **exalt the horn of the anointed** (me)."

***A Little Note:** <u>FEAR NOT</u> **is mentioned** <u>365 times</u> **in the bible one for every day of the year.**

CHAPTER 7

WHAT THE LORD SHARED WITH ME

JUNE 7, 1995

After singing "What A Healing Jesus" and confessing yesterday's promises, this is what the Lord shared with me:

Matthew 9:22 "Daughter, be of good comfort: **Thy faith** hath made thee whole."

Job 22:25-30 "Ye, the almighty shall be thy defense and thou shalt have plenty of silver. For then shalt thou have thy delight in the Almighty and shalt lift up thy face unto God. Thou shalt make thy prayer unto him and he shall hear thee and thou shalt pay thy vows. Thou shalt also decree (state) a thing and it shall be established unto thee, and the light shall shine upon thy ways. When men are cast down, then thou shalt say, there is lifting up; and he (you) shall save the humble person. He (you) shall deliver the island of the innocent: and it is delivered by the pureness of thine hands."

These scriptures showed me that God:

- God will defend me

- I will delight in God

- I will pray and God will hear me

- I will pay my vows

- I will state a thing and it will be established

- God's light will shine on my ways

- I will because of God's light to me be able to say to others that God can lift them up also.

- That God will use me for the humble, innocent persons because my trust is in him.

As I was praying to God, He let me hear someone from Trinity Broadcasting sing, "You'll Never Thirst Again" another special song I had learned and used to minister to others with. I have living water (God's Word) flowing through me. I'll never thirst again for God's word is over me and in me.

God continues giving me more scriptures to minister to me today:

Mark 10:27 "With men it is impossible but not with God; for with God all things are possible."

Mark 16:15-18 "Go into all the world and preach the gospel to every creature. He that believeth and is baptized shall be saved: but he that believeth not shall be damned. And these signs shall follow them that believe: In my name shall they cast out devils: they shall speak with new tongues: They shall take up serpents: and if they drink any deadly thing, it shall not hurt them: they shall lay hands on the sick, and they shall recover."

John 1:12 "But as many as received him to them gave he power to become the Sons (Daughters) of God, even to them that believe on his name."

John 1:13 "Which were born, not of blood nor of the will of the flesh, nor of the will of man, but of God."

Acts 11:16b "John indeed baptized with water; but ye shall be baptized with the Holy Ghost."

II Corinthians 1:2-24 "Grace be to you and peace from God our Father, and from the Lord Jesus Christ. Blessed be God, even the Father of our Lord Jesus Christ, the Father of mercies, and **the God of all comfort**: Whom comforteth us in all our tribulation, that we may be able to comfort them which are in any trouble, by the comfort wherewith ourselves are comforted of God.

For as the sufferings of Christ abound in us, so our con-solation also aboundeth by Christ. And whether we be afflicted, it is for your consolation and salvation, which is effectual in the enduring of the same sufferings which we also suffer: or whether we be comforted, it is for your consolation and salvation. And our hope of you is steadfast, knowing, that as ye are partakers of the sufferings, so shall ye be also of the consolation.

For we would not, brethren, have you ignorant of our trouble which came to us in Asia, that we were pressed out of measure, above strength, insomuch that we despaired even of life: **But we had the sentence of death in ourselves, that we should not trust in ourselves, but in God which raiseth the dead: Who delivered us from so great a death and doth deliver: in whom we trust that he will yet deliver us:** Ye also helping together by prayer for us, that for the gift bestowed upon us by the means of many persons thanks may be given by many on our behalf. **For our rejoicing is this, the testimony of our conscience, that in simplicity and godly sincerity, not with fleshly wisdom, but by the grace of God,** we have had our conversation in the world, and more abundantly to you ward.

For we write none other things unto you, than what ye read or acknowledge: and I trust ye shall acknowledge even to the end; As also ye have acknowledged us in part, that we are your rejoicing even as ye also are ours in the day of the Lord Jesus. And in this confidence I was minded to come unto you before, that ye might have a second benefit: And the pass by you into Macedonia, and to come again out of Macedonia unto you, and of you to be brought on my way toward Judea. When therefore was thus minded, did I use lightness? Or the things that I purpose, do I purpose according to the flesh, that with me there should be yea, yea, and nay, nay? But as God is true, our word toward you was not yea and nay, **For the Son of God, Jesus Christ,** who was preached among you by us, even by me and Silvanus and Timotheus, was not yea and nay, but in him was yea. **For all the promises for God in Him are yea, and in Him Amen, (so be it). Unto the Glory of God By Us. Now He which Stablisheth Us With You In Christ, and Hath Anointed Us, Is God: Who Hath Also Sealed Us and Given The Earnest of the Spirit In Our Hearts.**

Moreover I call God for a record upon my soul, that to spare you I came not as yet unto Corinth. **Not for that we have dominion over your faith, but are helper of your joy:** <u>For By Faith Ye Stand</u>."

II Corinthians 5:7 "For We Walk By Faith Not By Sight."

II Corinthians 4:18 "While we look **not** at the things which are seen, but at the things **which are not seen**: for the things which are seen are temporal; but the **things which are not seen are eternal.**

II Corinthians 4:6 & 7 "For God who commanded the light to shine out of darkness hath shined in our hearts, to give the light of the knowledge of **the glory of God (Glory means goodness in its purest form)** in the face of Jesus Christ (Christ means anointed). But, we have this treasure (the anointing) in earthen vessels, that the excellency of the power may be of God and not of us."

Mark 8:33 "Get Thee Behind Me Satan For Thou Savourest Not The Things of God, But The Things That Be Of Men."

Mark 9:23 "Jesus said unto him, "If thou (you) canst believe, all things are possible to him that believeth."

Stand In What God Says

Direction for Praise and Worship for me….

To make sure God wanted me to praise Him at this time, I asked Him if this was of Him to let me see it in the other Bible on my table. Sure enough I opened the other Bible and it opened to the same scripture.

II Chronicles 5:13-14 "It came to pass as the trumpeters and singers were **as one**, to make **one** sound to be heard in **praising** and **thanking** the Lord; and when they **lifted up their voices** with trumpets and cymbals and instruments of music, and **praised** the Lord, **Saying for He is good: for His MERCY endureth forever:** that **then the house was filled with a cloud,** (refers to the Holy Spirit) even the house of the Lord so that the **priests could not stand to minister** by reason of the cloud; For the **glory (goodness in purest form) of the Lord had filled the house of God."**

So I proceeded to Praise and Worship and thank the Lord for His goodness and mercy towards me.

CHAPTER 8

JUST ME AND GOD

JUNE 8, 1995

The days were passing on and soon I would be able to see Dr. Popwell the new chiropractor.

God and I, however, have been really communicating, as you know by reading my book.

Today the pain in my back was really bothering me and I really wanted to change my appointment with the new chiropractor from tomorrow to today since I hadn't been able to get an appointment with him all this time. But God's timing is better than ours, so I said, "O.K. God it's me and you again…no one else, so help me through this day." And God was faithful.

Isaiah 53:5 "But He was wounded for our transgressions he was bruised for our iniquities the chastisement of our peace was upon him; and **with his stripes we are healed.**"

I Peter 2:24 "Who his (Jesus) own self bare our sins in

his own body on the tree, that we, being dead to sins, should live unto righteousness: **by whose stripes ye were healed."**

God has not forsaken me. He revealed his truths to me and let me know he was my healer.

Healing according to Isaiah and Peter occurred in the present and past. There is no need in the future because we're with God and everything is perfect.

Note: Transgression = wickedness and rebellion Personal Wholeness – mental, psychological, physical and spiritual flows from conversion.

Hosea 6:1 "Come and let us return to the Lord; for he hath torn, and he will heal us."

Luke 10:56 "for the Son of man is not come to destroy men's lives but to save them." (speaking of Jesus)

John 16:33 "These things I have spoken unto you (Marilyn) that in me you might have peace. In the world ye shall have tribulation: but be of good cheer; I have overcome the world."

Acts 26: 16-18 "But rise and stand upon thy feet; for I have appeared unto thee **for this purpose,** to make **thee a minister and a witness both of** these things which thou hast seen and of these things in the which I will appear unto thee; delivering thee from the people and from the Gentiles unto whom now I sent thee. **To open their eyes and to turn them from darkness to light, and from**

the power, of Satan unto God, that they may receive forgiveness of sins, and inheritance among them which are sanctified by <u>faith </u>that is in me.

Philippians 4:19 "But **my God shall supply all your needs** according to His riches in Glory."

John 3:16-18 "For God so loved the world that He gave His only begotten Son, that whosever (you) believeth in Him should not perish, but have everlasting life, for God sent not His Son into the world to condemn the world: but that the world through Him might be saved, he that believeth on Him is not condemned: but he that believeth not is condemned already, because he hath not believed in the name of the only begotton Son of God."

Today the Lord showed me that He would use me in the lives of other people to help them to understand God's love and how to, **Walk With Him By Faith.** That walking in faith is just as important today as it was in biblical times.

The song on Trinity Broadcasting played in the background Praise God: **"I've Got A Feeling Everything Is Going To Be Alright"**

CHAPTER 9

MY UNEXPECTED MIRACLE HAPPENED TODAY

JUNE 9, 1995

Well, today I finally get to go met with my new Christian chiropractor.

While I was waiting to be seen by the new chiropractor, which was later on today, I remembered that I was to pray for my healing.

Remember back on June 7th God gave me this wisdom…

Mark 10:27 "With men it is impossible but not with God; for with God all things are possible."

As I lay in bed this morning on my back, the bone that was out of place and still resting on my nerve was causing me great pain. I called out to the Lord and quoted the scripture He gave me just recently. **"Daughter thy faith has made thee whole." I confessed this scripture out loud. Then**

I remembered I needed to <u>receive my healing</u>**. So I said with all I believed "I receive my healing now in the name of Jesus Christ.** Then I felt a sharp pain in my back and **felt the bone move into place** a few moments later the pain lifted. My vertebra was resting on a nerve causing me to feel pain and also having a lack of blood flow to the left side of my head, which also cause me not to be able to see very well out of my left eye nor be able to have strength in my left arm. But God moved that old vertebra back into place. **This was the beginning of God restoring health back to me**. **This was the key to my healing.** This is what the original chiropractor didn't address. **THIS WAS THE BEGINNING OF MY MIRACLE**. How do I know that the bone had moved? Not only because I felt it move but also because when I saw the new chiropractor, Dr. Popwell, he took an x-ray and the bone was back in place. This was a conformation that God had actually moved my bone this morning. Praise God. From this day forward I never had to sleep with my left arm straight up over my head. And I could sleep on my left side again. This was the true beginning of the healing process that would take place in me for the next several months. The bone moving off my nerve was the **key** to my body being healed. Thank you God.

My appointment with the doctor wasn't till after dinner so I had the whole day for more promises from God.

Today's Scriptures for Me:

Luke 12:22-24 "And he (Jesus) said unto his disciples,

Therefore I say unto you, **Take no thought for your life, what ye shall eat; neither for the body, what ye shall put on.** The life is more than meat and body is more than raiment. **Consider the ravens;** for they neither sow nor reap; which neither have storehouse nor barn; and **God feedeth them: how much more are ye better than the fowls?** And which of you with taking thought can add to his stature (height) one cubit? If ye then be not able to do that thing which is least, why take ye though for the rest? **Consider the lilies how they grow:** they toil not, they spin not; and yet I say unto you, that Solomon in all his glory was not arrayed (robed) like one of these. If then God so clothe the grass, which is to-day in the field, and to-morrow is cast into the oven; how much more will he clothe you, o ye of little faith? And **seek not ye what ye shall eat, or what ye shall drink, neither be ye of doubt-ful mind.** For all these thing do the nations of the world seek after: and **your Father knoweth that ye have need of these things.**

But **rather seek ye the kingdom of God** and **all these things shall be added unto you. Fear not,** little flock; for it is your Father's good pleasure to give you the kingdom. Sell that ye have, and give alms; provide yourselves bags which wax not old, **a treasure in the heavens that faileth not,** where no thief approacheth, neither moth corrupteth. **For where your treasure is, there will your heart be also."**

Through Luke 12:22-24, God was telling me that all I really need is to seek Him and He will provide for me all that I need.

Acts 10:15B "What God hath cleansed that call not thou uncommon"

(If I was made a little crooked like the tree and God heals me don't call me uncommon I am still worth His love and good health.)

Jeremiah 30:17A "For I will restore health unto thee."

Hebrews 10:36 "For **you have need of patience** that, after ye have **done the will of God,** ye **might receive the promise."**

I Corinthians 10:13 "There hath no temptation taken you but such as is common to man but **God is faithful,** who will not suffer you to be tempted **above what you are able,** but will with the temptation also **make a way of escape, that ye may be able to bear it."**

Philippians 4:19 "But My God Shall Supply ALL Your Needs According To His Riches In Glory By Christ Jesus."

Luke 1:17 "For With God NOTHING Shall Be Impossible."

Rejoice and Give Thanks to the Lord

Psalms 95 "Oh come, let us sing unto the Lord; let us make a joyful noise to the rock of our salvation. Let us come before his presence with thanksgiving, and make a joyful noise unto him with psalms. For the Lord, is a great God, and a great King above all gods. In his hand are the deep places of the earth: the strength of the hills is his also. The sea is his, and made it: and his hands formed the dry land. O come, let us worship and bow down: let us kneel before the Lord our maker. For he is our God; and we are the people of his pasture and the sheep of his hand. **Today if you will here his voice. Harden not your heart,** as in the day of temptation in the wilderness: when your fathers tempted me, proved me, and saw my work. Forty years long was I grieved with this generation, and said, "It is a **people that do err in their heart,** and they have not know my ways: Unto whom I swear in my wrath that **they should not enter into my rest."**

Through Psalm 95, God was showing me to listen for His voice and follow Him.

Psalms 148:11 "The Lord taketh pleasure in them that **fear him, in those that hope in his mercy."**

Mark 5:34 "Daughter Thy Faith Hath Made Thee Whole."

Isaiah 60:1-2 "Arise and shine for the light has come and the glory of the Lord is risen upon thee, for behold, the darkness shall cover the earth and gross darkness the people: but the **Lord Shall Rise Upon Thee, And His Glory (goodness) Shall Be Seen Upon Thee."**

Micah 7:7 "Therefore I Will Look Unto The Lord: I

Will Wait For The God Of My Salvation My God Will Hear Me." (Resurrection power)

Micah 7:8 "Rejoice not against me, o mine enemy when I fall, I shall arise; when I sit in darkness, **The Lord Shall Be A Light Unto Me."**

Finally, I went to the chiropractor to get the results of the exam. I was scared. But, God is faithful, don't you know? He gave me that same scripture again **"Daughter THY FAITH hath mad thee whole."** But He gave me one more bit of direction. He showed me a scripture that said, **"Don't Be Afraid, Only Believe."**

God and His Provisions

Remember the tree God showed me at the very beginning of my story? Needless to say, I was fighting the good fight of FAITH. When I finally was able to see my new Christian chiropractor, Dr. Popwell, (God has such a sense of humor), he began to relate a story of a tree to me then explain my situation. I stopped him real quick and asked him if I could tell him what God showed me about a crooked tree 3 weeks before I came to him. Boy did the doctor's face drop. I had stolen his thunder. He proceeded to tell me that he just took a picture of two trees the past weekend while he was out on the golf course. He sent his assistant to get the picture of the trees that he took. He said that he wanted me to have it. That he was going to use it in his office, but because God shared with me what he did about the bent tree and the straight tree, Dr. Popwell thought that the picture should be given to me.

This is the picture Dr. Popwell gave me this today, June 9, 1995

He said that some people are just a little curvy and that they shouldn't be tampered with as I had been.... curvy, meaning, along my spinal column. He then told me that the first doctor tried to straighten me out as if I was a small child. That is what caused all my problems. Well, I was not a child but, well not that old, but not that young. Dr. Popwell told me I could get well even though my bones weren't perfectly inline. That the x-ray **did not** show any bones out of place (of course not. When the x-ray was taken, God had already moved the bone that morning, Praise God.) We never seemed to address the injured nerve for some reason. I don't think he even thought there was an injury there, but I did. God new also, but apparently God wanted the nerve to heal naturally and not be tampered with by any one.

My neck and shoulder and back muscles on my left side were in a spasm so massage therapy was in order. I was scared, " I thought, "Oh No", don't let anyone touch my neck. I might fall over again and not be able to move.

Healing Hands

I want to tell you a little about my massage therapist, Sharon. I had prayed, "Oh God, if I need massage therapy please send an angel."…Then Sharon walked into the room. She was a spirit-filled, born again woman who believed in healing. As she massaged me she relied on the presence of God to work through her hands. She encouraged me to rest my head in her hands as if her hands were the hands of Jesus. She was what I called (my special angel from God). She came over my house many times for my massage therapy and would sometimes take me out for walks. She encouraged me to not be afraid. She was also from Wisconsin which made her more special to me because we had just moved from Wisconsin and I just loved the people there.

In the future, when my massage therapist would come to the house, and the time came for my neck to be relaxed, she would always say, "Place your head in my hands and think that you are placing your head in the hands of Jesus." That really helped relax me.

I was also instructed by the doctor to listen to a tape on forgiveness so that I wouldn't harbor any hatred or anger towards the previous doctor who got me into this condition. He told me that by forgiving, it would help me to concentrate on my healing and not the anger. Anyway, I thought… hey no way, I'm mad. But, I took the instruction and believe me, sitting in anger would have not helped me one bit.

I had numerous massages and my new lady massage therapist, Sharon, told my husband to massage me in-between the sessions I had with her. The reason being is that my muscles needed to remember to relax. She showed him how to do the massage. She said, if he didn't massage me every night that I would never be well. So there was my hubby massaging me for 7 months straight. That's right every day for 7 months. What a blessing he was. I would get a numbing feeling up into my head every day and when he would massage me, the blood would flow and the numbness would go away, only to come back the next day. He would call me his windup doll.

My husband, John, who massaged me every night, never complained. He took care of our dog and cat and fed us all. He encouraged me every step of the way. He took me to church every Wednesday and Sunday. He prayed many times with me, walked with me on the beach picking up shells many days and took me with him to shop for food, even though I could barely get myself out of the house. I couldn't even lift a thing. He walked with me in patience and love, encouraging me all the way, as God was healing me.

One day, I felt really faint after my massage with my therapist and she said, "Oh, let's go out for a walk." She put my dog, Candy, on a leash and we all walked the complex together. I felt ten times better coming back home. So everyday after this, I would exercise in the morning and in the afternoon. Candy and I would walk around the complex. Of course, I prayed and continued my walk with the Lord.

My husband was also instructed to take me over to the pool and encourage me to swim to help the movement of my muscles.

I couldn't go shopping, I couldn't lift anything, my eyesight was starting to get better a little at a time because my nerve was healing, and my muscles were starting to relax, a little at a time. I couldn't clap more than a few times or my muscles and shoulder would freeze up on me. Many times I was in a lot of pain after the massage therapist would work on me. I used a lot of ice packs. I slept a lot in the afternoon and even after my husband would massage me, I would fall right to sleep every night. But, I had learned that sleeping was good for you because that is when your body has a good chance to heal itself. I exercised every day with my videotape, walking mostly and some regular exercises with another tape and of course walking with my dog, Candy.

Candy And Me

God even used Candy to help encourage me to move my arm. I am left handed…so when Candy would come over to me and want to play, the first time I said, "Candy, I don't think I can throw the ball, but I will try."…And therein was the moving of my arm once again as therapy. After that, I played with my sweet loving dog, Candy, as often as she wanted.

CHAPTER 10

GOD GAVE ME HELP

JUNE 10, 1995

Today, God gave me help from a Christian calendar that was given to me as a present.

John 21:9 & 15 "They saw a fire of burning coals there with fish on it, and some bread…When they finished eating, Jesus said to Simon Peter, "Simon, son of John, do you truly love me more than these?"

"The Master Psychiatrist (Jesus) led Peter to face his most traumatic memory, and used a charcoal fire to cauterize and heal Peter's pain and shame. With the sting removed, Peter would be able to **use that burning memory, not as a curse which crippled, but as a spark to ignite him to deeper devotion."**

Isn't God good? He even helped me in my memory of this traumatic situation to use it, not as a hurtful crippling thing in my life, but as a spark, an excitement to walk with God deeper than before thereby. I will find joy and freedom to go on.

There are a few people God used through this time of healing. There was my pastor and how he prayed for me when I had a very bad pain in my head. That pain left and never came back.

The first person that God used in my life was my husband who held me up in prayer many times and was the most encouraging and loving person throughout this whole ordeal. You of course, read about how much he did for me previously.

The other special person God brought into my life was Oral Roberts. I had told God one day that I would love to see Oral Roberts in person. Well God brought Oral Roberts to a church near where we lived. Not really feeling well enough to go out, I pushed myself to go to church anyway. After Oral Roberts preached, he said, "God is giving me a Word of knowledge. I don't know what this means, but someone has a frozen shoulder and God is healing you right now." Who is that? Please stand up. The person was me. I could feel the healing taking place. I stood up and after I left the service my shoulder that would not relax no matter how many massages I had, was now relaxed and never went back into that frozen state again. Praise God.

CHAPTER 11

"THE PERFECT WOMAN"

JUNE 13, 1995

AFTER PRAYER, IN THE MORNING.

A woman knelt in prayer and being in anguish she cried out to God. "Dear Lord, I can't compete in this world. I am just a simple woman. I don't have perfect hair or perfect teeth, a perfect figure. I want so much to fit in with the world that asks for perfection. I want to be loved and appreciated and needed. Oh God, please do something. Change me."

"My Dear Child", replied the Lord, "**To me you are simply wonderful.** I accept you just as you are. I knew you when you were in your mother's womb, and I have you engraved upon the palm of my hand. Each part of you was created in my image and I am changing you daily.

But you see, I work differently than the world. I work from

the inside out and deep within you, I see the beginning of perfection."

Ephesians 2:8, 9 and 10 "For by grace are you saved through **Faith**; and that not of yourself: it is a gift of God. Not by works, lest any man should boast. For we are his workmanship created in Christ Jesus unto good works, which God hath before ordained that we should walk in them."

Romans 10: 4, 9 & 10 "For Christ is the end of the law for righteousness to every one that believeth." "That if thou shalt confess with thy mouth the Lord Jesus, and shalt believe in thine heart that God hath raised him from the dead, thou shalt be saved." "For with the heart man believeth unto righteousness; and with the mouth confession is made unto salvation."

Philippians 4:4-8 "There is one body, and one Spirit, even as ye are called in one hope of your calling; One Lord, One faith, one baptism, One God and Father of all, who is above all, and through all, and in you all. But unto every one of us is given grace according to the measure of the gift of Christ. Wherefore he saith, When he ascended up on high, he led captivity captive, and gave gifts unto men."

CHAPTER 12

RETAINING YOUR HEALING

JUNE 14, 1995

Sometimes we receive our healing and things are going really well and then, all of a sudden, it feels like no healing took place at all. That is when we need to retain our healing. I didn't know this, but God knew that I needed to learn this truth.

Here I was gaining ground and healing taking place. But, oh no! There are always curves thrown our way that are not from God. They are thrown our way so that we will lose our Faith in God's Word and His provisions.

I was on the road to healing. But, then the questions, temptations and doubts came flooding in. Maybe I'm not doing the right thing. Why would I question God? I told you that I went to swim in the pool to help with my muscle problems. There I ran into a girl that I had met previously. She was lying on a raft and her boyfriend was with her. She started to tell me about her neck and problems with her muscles in almost the same area I was having trouble. She said she was feeling fine. The doctor gave her pain pills and now she is feeling better. Pain pills seemed to be an easy solution (doubt). But, not for me, I thought. Pain pills only mask the problem. Next, was the new medical facility they put up right by the supermarket we went to. Of course, it was open to the public for a tour of the facility. As I walked through the place, I started to question if maybe I should go to a regular doctor. After all, I am not completely well. (Doubt again) By the time I left there, I had decided to trust what God was leading me to do.

Today the Lord showed me how to retain (keep) my healing and to keep his promises ever before me.

The mail came and I received "The Voice of Victory" magazine. It said right in the front **"How to Survive the Counter Attack"** related to retaining healing. I love the teaching of Kenneth Copeland so I started to read this article.

Retaining Healing

Keep God's Promises Before Your Eyes:

Mark 5:34 "Daughter thy **FAITH** hath made thee whole go in peace and be whole of thy plague."

II Corinthians 10:5 "Casting down imaginations and every high thing that exalts the knowledge of God."

Job 11:16, 17 "Because thou shalt forget thy misery and remember it as waters that pass away and thine age shall be clearer than the noonday thou shalt shine forth, thou shalt be as the morning."

Psalms 29:11 "The Lord will give strength unto his people the Lord will bless his people with peace."

Zechariah 10:12 "And I will strengthen them in the Lord and they shall walk up and down in his name." (Removal of oppression and restore)

Psalms 103 "Bless the Lord, O my soul: and all that is within me bless his holy name.

Bless the Lord, O my soul, and **forget not all his benefits**:

Who forgiveth all thine iniquities; who healeth all thy diseases;

Who redeemeth thy life from destruction; who crowneth thee with lovingkindness and tender mercies:

Who **satisfieth thy mouth with good things; so that thy youth is renewed like the eagle's**

The **Lord executeth righteousness and judgment for all that are oppressed.**

He made know his ways unto Moses, his acts unto the children of Israel.

The Lord is merciful and gracious, slow to anger, and plenteous in mercy.

He will not always chide (strive with us): neither will he keep his anger forever.

He hath not dealt with us after our sins; nor rewarded us according to our iniquities.

For as the heavens is high above the earth, so **great is his mercy toward them that fear him**.

As far as the east is from the west, so far hath **he removed our transgressions from us**.

Like as a father pitieth his children, so the Lord pitieth them that fear him.

For he knoweth our frame; he remembereth that we are dust. As for man, his days are as grass: as a flower of the field, so he flourisheth. For the wind passeth over it, and it is gone; and the place thereof shall know it no more.

But the mercy of the Lord is from everlasting to everlasting upon them that fear him and his righteousness unto children's children; For such as keep his covenant, and to those that remember his commandments to do them.

The Lord hath prepared his throne in the heavens; and his kingdom ruleth over all.

Bless the Lord, ye his angels that excel in strength, that do his commandments, hearkening unto the voice of his word.

Bless ye the Lord, all ye his hosts; ye ministers of his, that do his pleasure.

Bless the Lord, all his works in all places of his dominion: bless the Lord, O my soul (mind, will and emotions)".

John 5:14 "Behold, thou art made whole."

Matthew 9:22 "Daughter be of good comfort thy faith hath made thee whole."

Jeremiah 30:17 "For I will restore health unto thee: I will heal thee of thy wounds saith the Lord."

Hebrews 10:35 "Cast not away therefore your confidence which has recompense of great reward."

Surviving Counter Attack

- Confess you are healed by the stripes of Jesus and your healing date.

- Put God's word first place in your life.

- Keep focused on the promises God has given you.

- Thank the Lord for providing your healing:

Isaiah 53:5 "Thank you Lord for providing healing for me. By Faith I receive that provision now, in Jesus name. I set myself in agreement with your word which says: "By His stripes I was healed."

Speak to the problem. Come against the mountain.

Mark 11:22-23 "And Jesus answering saith unto them, "Have faith in God.""

"For verily I say unto you, That whosoever, shall **say** unto this mountain, Be thou removed, and be thou cast into the sea; and **shall not doubt in his heart, but shall believe** that those things which he saith shall come to pass, he shall have whatsoever he saith."

Praise God. There is power in praise.

Psalms 8:1 & 2…I kept this instruction of Surviving the Counter Attack and all these scriptures in my bathroom where I would read them every day out loud to keep my victory of healing in the Lord.

I don't walk bent over, the problem had to do with the alignment of my bones that still may not be perfectly straight, but by looking at me you could never tell.

One More Healing

Just a little side note to my healing. My tailbone had been moved out of place 20 years before this accident. All this time I wasn't able to sit except to cross my legs and lean to the right. I wasn't able to sit up and watch television I had to lay down on my side. I couldn't lift anything heavy. Yes, I had sought medical attention within these 20 years, one from a chiropractor. The tailbone had move out of place and was sitting totally sideways. He told me that only professional people would go for an operation to remove it. But, that I could live with it the way it was and I did for many years. When we were in Wisconsin, I went to another chiropractor for something else and somehow or another my tailbone moved and was irritating me and causing a lump that would get red and hot and then go away and come back again and again. Eventually, we moved from Wisconsin to Florida where I had this accident. Guess what God did for me as a healing bonus?

I said, "honey, guess what I just realized? my tailbone problem is gone. I can sit straight up. I don't need to lie down to watch television and I can lift up things that I couldn't before. I could sit Indian style (sit with my legs crossed on the floor). The irritation is gone. I am healed, I told him." My tailbone problem cleared up after 20 years of difficulty. I told my husband that I don't know how it happened and I don't know where in the world my tailbone is and I don't care. From this time forward, I have never had a problem with my tailbone. It has been 18 years since it happened and I still don't care where my tailbone went. All I know is that God healed me. It just goes to show you that, "All things work together for good to them that love God and are called according to his purposes." Romans 8:28

CONCLUSION

Remember the man I told you about from the Pipeline To Jesus meeting; how he handed me a dollar bill with all seven's on it? The number Seven in the bible represents perfection. He also told me that I would be receiving a miracle. The total manifestation of my healing didn't come for Seven months. That was December 1995. I received my total complete miracle. Praise God.

Each day for seven months my husband massaged my shoulder and upper back area. My massage therapist worked on me for seven months as well. I walked with Candy, my dog and exercised every day. I went swimming as I could. I praised and worshipped the Lord and kept myself in the Word of God. I really couldn't sing very well because of the injury that affected my muscles, but God even restored my ability to sing. I was able to see clear again. My muscles finally relaxed. The pain was gone from the damaged nerve in my back.

One day I went to the supermarket by myself and was able to reach up and take groceries off the shelves. I was so excited and thankful to God that I wanted to just start dancing and rejoicing all over the store. What a sight that would have been to the people shopping. No one really knew the joy that came over me as I was walking and moving because God had healed me.

Romans 1:15 & 17

"For I am not ashamed of the gospel of Christ: For it is THE POWER OF GOD UNTO SALVATION TO EVERYONE THAT BELIEVETH to the Jews first and also to the Greek.

For therein is the righteousness of God revealed from FAITH TO FAITH as it is written: THE JUST SHALL LIVE BY FAITH."

What happened to me was beyond my control and was meant for evil to hurt me and destroy me. Yet, through it all, I found God to be greater and His Word to be the substance of my faith. He led me on a journey through the pain, through the fear, through the times of bitterness and resentment to a place of victory where peace rules my heart and I am free of the evil that was cast upon me.

My journey was not by sight for had it been, it would have destroyed me, but rather by faith to restore me. I listened to the voice of God as He spoke to me in the bible and believed Him. If you turn back to page 24 and read the last scripture the Lord gave me you will read Acts 26:16-18 talking about making me a minister and a witness to others. It was about one year or so that I was ordained as a minister through Faith Christian Fellowship of Tulsa,

Oklahoma. I have also witnessed to many about what God has done in my life and now to you about my awesome healing through this book. God has kept all his promises to me.

Let me encourage you also to walk by faith, holding onto the Word of God as your confidence and assurance that God is with you and wants to deliver you from every trial. "Many are the afflictions of the righteous but God delivers them from them all." Believing God is the key to activating your faith and realizing your victory.

God Bless You In Your Walk Of Faith

My Prayer

11/12/02

God, you know my heart and all the lies and
falsehoods that live within my soul.

I want to do your will and minister for you – Yet this
snare of deception I believe seems to take hold of me.

Help – Jesus – clear the paths that we may
dwell and be blessed and be a blessing.

God…..

The deception lies within your soul,

Based on hurts of long ago.

Sitting and pondering on what life should bring,

Keeping bound and covered with sin.

As you sit beside the brook,

Know what is and stop and look.

And see what plans I have for thee.

They are based on the lost and found,
They are based on thoughts all around.

Some are good and some are bad,
Some filled with fear of what you had.

Time flees by and you will know,
What truth is within your soul.

No more to hinder, no more to fear,
A new course in time, holding nothing near.

For all the leaves have shed their brilliancy,
Leaving you wandering and wondering where to be.

Stop, look and listen to the sounds,
Look there all on sold ground.

The winds have blown, so stop and see
What happened to the tree?

The devil cast his hurtful song,
But, with me you belong.

Stop and listen to the whistling of the trees,
The hurts, the fears of all the leaves.

Come sit and take my hand
And walk with me through the land.

Stop and look at all around
Are there leaves left on the ground?

Saddened hearts and woeful cries,
Linger on till they die.

Shine on; shine on amidst the pain,
No more to walk on leaves filled rain.

For truth will shine within your days,
No more to look to other's ways.
Look up, to the Lord,
His peace restored,
Within your brokenness,
There is so much more.

Stand up to shine
Within the night.
The morning breaks
And so much more
For peace I give and then restore.

Shine on oh fair one of the night,
Don't forget who shined the light.
Stand up; stand up for all to see
That light shines from me.

Do not fret or even fear,
For I hold you very dear.
Place your feet on solid ground,
And free the others as they are found.

Shine on, shine on within the night
Make your plea to all that's right.
Be of good courage and do not fear
The time of testing is so very clear.

Stand within this test of time,
Forever shine always be mine.
Keep the peace and stand tall.
Don't look to those that fall.

For many trees will shed their light,
Of glimmering hope, for that's right.
Don't stand within these shadow walls,
And listen to their beckoning call.

For their leaves will take a turn of color

and leave others with stormy weather.
Shine on; shine on for all to see
For you are planted as God's seed.
Shine on, stand the test of time,
Forever my love
You are always mine.

Micah 7:5 "Trust ye not in a friend, put
not your confidence in a guide."
Marilyn Marinelli

Gallery of Christian Poems

LOST DREAMS

I lost my dreams like dirty clothes,
They began to get gray and very old.
The dreams I had used to shine,
But now, it seems I'm carrying a load.

Too much time has past, you see,
There is nothing left for me.
But wait just a minute, can it be
God, hasn't stopped, He set me free.

Free from the toil of a dreary day,
Free to be me, even if you go away.
For I have my dreams,
God has given them to me.

God: "My dreams are your tomorrows,
They are hidden in time,
They are there if you want them to be,
They are measured like the sands of the sea."

Marilyn Marinelli

SNARES OF DECEPTION

The deception lies within your soul,
Based on hurts of long ago.
Sitting and pondering on what life should bring,
Keeping you bound and covered with sin.

As you sit beside the brook,
Know what is and stop and look,
And see what plans I have for thee.

They are based on the lost and found,
They are based on thoughts all around.
Some are good and some are bad,
Some filled with fear of what you had.

Time flees by and you will know,
What truth is within your soul.
No more to hinder, no more to fear,
A new course in time, holding nothing near.

For all the leaves have shed their brilliancy,
Leaving you wandering and wondering where to be.
Stop, look and listen to the sounds,
Look there all on sold ground.

The winds have blown, so stop and see

What happened to the tree?

The devil cast his hurtful song,

But, with me you belong.

Stop and listen to the whistling of the trees,

The hurts, the fears of all the leaves.

Come sit and take my hand,

And walk with me through the land.

Stop and look at all around,

Are there leaves left on the ground?

Saddened hearts and woeful cries,

Linger on till they die.

Shine on, shine on amidst the pain

No more to walk on leaves filled with rain.

For truth will shine with in your days,

No more to look to others ways.

Look up to the Lord,
His peace restored,
Within your brokenness
There is so much more.

"Stand Up To Shine"

Marilyn Marinelli

SHINE ON

Shine on, shine on amidst the pain,
No more to walk on leaves filled rain.
For truth will shine within your days,
No more to look to other's ways.

Look up, to the Lord,
His peace restored,
Within your brokenness,
There is so much more.

Stand up to shine,
Within the night.
The morning breaks
And so much more,
For peace I give and then restore.

Shine on, oh fair one, of the night,
Don't forget who shined the light.
Stand up, stand up for all to see,
That light shines from me.

Do not fret or even fear,
For I hold you very dear.

Place your feet on solid ground,
And free the others as they are found.

Shine on, shine on, within the night,
Make your plea to all that's right.
Be of good courage and do not fear,
The time of testing is so very clear.

Stand within this test of time,
Forever shine always be mine.
Keep the peace and stand tall,
Don't look to those that fall.

For many trees will shed their light,
Of glimmering hope, for all that's right.
Don't stand within these shadow walls,
And listen to their beckoning call.

For their leaves will take a turn of color,
And leave others with stormy weather.
Shine, shine on, for all to see,
For you are planted as God's seed.

Shine on, stand the test of time,
Forever my love, you are always mine.

Micha 7:5 "Trust ye not in a friend, put not your confidence in a guide."

Marilyn Marinelli

As I Was On The Cross

I saw you as I was on the cross.
Your sadness and your pain.
I knew you needed hope,
That your life was filled with shame.

I knew you would be weary.
And would lose all hope to fear.
But, my child, I tell you
My salvation will adhere.

For every sorrow, pain and fear,
And for every doubtful thought,
I died for you that day.
Your salvation, I have bought.

Marilyn Marinelli

ARE ANIMALS IN HEAVEN?

In Genesis, we read how God
created the sky and the seas,
And then He created
the fish, the birds and the bees.

All the animals were created one by one,
And when He was through, and when He was done,
He created Adam to name them all,
Giving them names great and small.

So why would the animals that did no wrong
Not be with God when their days are gone?
If the lion will lie down with the lamb,
And Jesus, on a white horse, will come for man,
Then how can one say without any doubt,
That the animals would be left out?
Think About It

Marilyn Marinelli

Quiet Hours

In the silence of the quiet hours,
in the presence of a new dawn,
I bow down upon my knees,
for bringing me life reborn.

Taking off all the shackles,
letting my spirit free.
I give all the thanks to Jesus,
for giving His love to me.

Written By Marilyn Marinelli

Published as an entry sign to the Christian Conference Center (walk of prayer) off Hwy. 40 Ocala, Florida

A LITTLE WORD

Sitting by the side of the brook
I took a chance to look
At the paper in my hand
Which wasn't so grand.

But as I sat by the water's edge,
I read the print and this is what it said,
"My dear friend, Jesus wants you to know,
that you are loved. He wants you to grow.

Don't be discouraged and do not fear,
For your time of deliverance is very near."

It seemed so apropos
that I read these lines today,
For I wanted to give up my life
But the words of the poet gave me hope to stay.

All that I needed, a word from God
A little hope of reflection that my life wasn't marred;
That I could go on and know I'd be set free,
So I bent on my knee for anyone to see.

I reflected and prayed that very day
And got up brand new and went on my way.
But before I left, I raised my head and with a sigh
said, "Thank you Lord for this poem from on high."

Marilyn Marinelli

TO SHARE IN YOUR LOVE

I got up this morning to praise you
Oh, most high,
Look, I got up to praise you
my God most high.

I was ordered by your spirit
from your throne above
to worship and praise you
and give you my love.

The showers of mercy
that flow from your throne,
encircles my heart
and leads me, never to roam.

For in the silence
of your enduring love,

I wake up this morning

to share in your love.

Marilyn Marinelli

When You Don't See the Hand of God

When you don't see the hand of God,
He is still there.
Just praise and pray through the clouds
Of loneliness and despair.

When you don't see God,
Have you walked on the road
Leading nowhere?

When you see that God isn't there,
Is it because you've left your 1st love, Jesus?
When you don't see God there, isn't He?
Is His arm too short that He cannot reach you?

And when you cry in the night,
Is not His hand a cup to hold your tears
And soothe your weary mind?

Where is God when you do not see His hand?
Why, right beside you, with outstretched hands.
His Spirit woos you back to Him,
Calling your name tonight

As your tear stained pillow lays by your head.
God is there to heal your dread.
Psalm 56 and "I will never leave you
or forsake you", saith the Lord.

Marilyn Marinelli

WATER ME LORD

MY PRAYER TO GOD

Water me Lord with your love.
Shower me with your Words from above.
Fill me Lord with you mercy and grace,
That I may behold your face.
Help me to grow and help me to see,
The wonder you have worked in me.

God's Answer

In the mist of your confusion, I am there
To wash away your every care.
When trouble seems to surround you,
Know my friend, that "I AM" is around you.
For trouble may come from every side
Yet, in my love you shall abide.
And every care that seems too hard to do,
My grace and love will see you through.

Marilyn Marinelli

DON'T GIVE UP

Don't give up your calling; don't give up God's grace,
Don't give up your smile; put on a happy face.
Don't give up your dreams and don't respond in doubt.
Just pick up all the pieces and give yourself a shout.

For when the enemy tries to defeat you
And you're feeling all alone.
Remember this my friend,
There is one that calls you His own.

He will not leave you in fear and doubt,
And will never let you fail.
He alone can take your fears.
With Him your dreams will sail.

Press on, oh man of grace and delight
And women in a dreadful fright.
For God will supply your every need,
If on Him, you do believe.

Marilyn Marinelli

Expectations

The expectations of the creatures wait,
For the sons of God, relying on their faith.

For the creature was made subject to man's vanity,
not willingly but still waiting for what is to be.

The creature itself shall also be,
Delivered from bondage into God's liberty.

Romans 8:19-21

Marilyn Marinelli

TEARDROPS FROM HEAVEN

The raindrops on your window
Are the teardrops from my angels
Crying for you
To let you know--
You are not alone.

My tears fill your broken heart
And comfort you in this time of need.
They are tears from heaven
That flow from my throne
To let you know--
You are not alone.

For when you are saddened
My heart cries for you
To send comfort to you.
Teardrops from heaven
For you this day
Streaks your window pane.

Tears from heaven
To help wash away the sorrow.
Teardrops from heaven--

Teardrops as I cry for you
To let you know …
I am close to healing your pain--

Teardrops from heaven,
Teardrops from heaven--
From God.

Marilyn Marinelli

WHO TRULY IS YOUR NEIGHBOR?

Who truly is your neighbor?",
Jesus asked me one day.
"Is it the people living next to you?",
Is what he had to say.

It's the person who stops to lend a hand,
When you truly have needs.
Like the person in Luke chapter ten,
Who fell among the thieves.

Some people passed him,
Refusing to heed his cry.
But, one stopped to help,
Without questioning why.

Who is your neighbor?"
Jesus asked me again that day.
"The one who will stop, And help me",
Was what I had to say.

Marilyn Marinelli

A Dog Without a Soul?

How could it be what some men say,
That the dog has no soul? No way!
How can God create them great and small,
And leave out the greatest gift of all?

When you look into their eyes
What is it that you see?
Isn't it caring and love,
And the essence of personality?

The soul is our Mind, Will and Emotions.
How could it be they have no devotion?
Have you ever noticed? Can it possibly be
That God gave them a soul like you and me?

So how can one say the dog has no soul,
When God created them to love and hold,

To show you love and lick your face,
As a loyal friend to the human race?

Marilyn Marinelli

You Can Be Born Again

Have you ever seen a stranger,
and wondered where they'd been?
What times they had,
what caused them to sin?

What are they hiding and carrying around?
Some act so silly or wear a frown.
How is it they don't let the Savior in,
To heal up their pain and remove all their sin?

What keeps them from calling to the one that can help?
What keeps them holding on to fear within themselves?
Won't they let the Savior in?
Don't they know He died for their sin?

The next time you see a stranger who hides
all of there sadness under much pride,
Tell them of Christ who can save them from sin.
Let them know they can be born again.

Marilyn Marinelli

COVERED

Covered over by a blinding light,

Twisting me to things not right,

Nor right for me.

I turned all about

Feeling alone and desperate for flight.

Covered in fear and all alone

Covered in ….cover, cover.

No where to roam.

Caged

By the blinding light.

Years of darkness, no light.

Sitting and hoping things would be right.

Shrouded in pain and fear, scream-

ing but no one could hear.

Covered

Wanted to be needed and loved, bound by fear.

Covered in shame for nothing I did.

Yet, living a lie, being hid.

Screaming in the night, running in the dark.

Screaming and yet no one hears.

Covered

By the light that was not right.
Covered, as if living in the night and
thinking it was all right.
Covered, and shrinking away to be
left by a darkening light.

"Beware that the light in you is not darkness."

Afraid and alone, covered.
Throw off the covers of this darkened light.
Throw off the shame of things not right.
Scream, scream for the struggle to be free.
Realizing that the light that is darkness is not right.
Covered

Deliver me Lord Jesus from this shame and deceit.
Give me the true light and help me up on my feet.
I shall not sit in this darkened light…
For it is not of you.
Covered

Where are you my fair one?

I am hidden in fear …. I am hid-
den because no one would hear.

I am hidden.
Hidden, from the ones that say they care.
Hidden, to live in heartache and despair.
I am hidden.
No one sees the beauty in me.
They tell me I'm wrong so they can be free.

HIDDEN

They are lost in broken dreams
Running from hurts that cannot be seen.

HIDDEN

These are the covers that kill their life
The covers of brokenness that are not alright.

DARKENED LIGHT

Hidden

This is not for you my child to sit in hidden array.
For it was not meant for you to stay hidden from the day.
My child of light, it will be alright as you sit by my side.
Never more to run and hide from the darkened light.
Rise up! rise and be heard.
Don't be ashamed of what you have heard.
Uncover yourself from this darkened state
I will walk with you in true light, if you have heard.

Lighting your path to a new life and way.
It's time to come out of this saddened array.
This is not for you my child to sit in hidden array.
For it was not meant for you to stay hidden from the day.
My child of light, it will be all right as you sit by my side,
Never more to run and hide from the darkened light.
Rise up rise and be heard.
Don't be ashamed of what you have heard.
Uncover yourself from this darkened state.
I will walk with you in true light, if you have heard.

Lighting your path to a new life and way.
It's time to come out of the saddened array.

COVERED, HIDDEN

Step out into the light of day,
Where we can plan each new day.
Don't sit with the lies of men
Stay away from those that walk in this sin.
Hidden state of darkened light.

Written by the leading of the Lord

Marilyn Marinelli
July 2005

I AM

The sadness that lingers within your soul,
Is musty & covered with hurts of old.
Time passes each day & fear & loneliness fills your mind.
Thought of sadness from unforgotten times.

Your dreariness of mind will be stopped of its strain.
Cannot you see I removed all the care?
Don't you know I'm with you when loneliness is there?

All you must do through this time of despair,
Is to know my friend, "I AM" is there.
"I AM" your tomorrows "I Am" all your peace.
"I AM" all your joy, "I AM" sweat release.

All your tomorrows will cover this fear.
Your sadness & sorrow will never be near.
The stress & the strain that has kept you bound,
Will be released & never be found.

Your tomorrows will fill a cup in time,
Of memories lost of a forgotten time.
So do not fear or fret, my child, my salvation draws near
For in this loss of time, my love will adhere.

I hear you in your dark despair.
There is never a time that "I AM" is not there.
For in your darkness, doubts & fears,
A new creature, I make you, throughout all your tears.

The times are past. A new light will shine,
Through your weary sadness of heart & broken time.
I repair all the worry & fear & frets.
For "I AM" your Savior. There will be no regrets.

A time of renewing like fresh falling rain.
Will cause you to grow & remove all the strain.
A new heart I'll give you. A new walk in time,
Filled with my blessings, you'll always be mine.

I'll give you new tomorrows that will shine as a light.
Everything will be better. I'll make things all right.
No more will you wander on roads of despair,
For I have overcome this time of care.

So don't forget who is holding your hand,
"I AM" is with you as you walk thru this land.
"I AM" all your tomorrows, "I AM" all your peace,
"I AM" all your strength, "I AM" your sweet release.

Marilyn Marinelli

Freedom! Freedom! Shouting In My Heart

A shout of Freedom that no one hears.
For the Freedom that I found
Is within my heart.
Placed in me from God above
To give me a brand new start.

Freedom from discouragement.
Freedom, from all fear.
Freedom from past hurts and shame.
Freedom all the year.

"A new person I have made you.
Free to be your own.
With my guiding hand,
You'll never be alone.

I'll take that old stony heart of yours
And melt it and make it new;
And give you joy and happiness
That all had said not true.

I'll turn your captivity
Right before your eyes
And give you peace of mind
I'll never, never lie.

Freedom rings within your soul
A gift from God above,
So that you can always be
Abiding in His love.

Marilyn Marinelli

THE PRESSURES OF LIFE

The pressures of life seem to be spent,
on life's passing events.
The past rears it's head on the things,
that should be gone and dead.

But, in our times of loneliness and despair,
we find ourselves as if we were there.
Cries and sobbing and reflecting on things,
that leave us remembering the sadness it brings.

Oh, to forget the past hurts and pains.
A love of light to ease the strain.
If only to be changed into a newness of time.
A new birth that God says is mine.

Then ever so grateful, I always will be.
Free at last to be really me.

Marilyn Marinelli

A New Creature

I know your hurts and bruises too,
the tongue that says you can never be new.
But, this I say to all this day,
that a new creature you'll be in every way.

Time will pass and you will be,
a new creature who stands in me.
Full of peace and love divine,
full of compassion forever mine.

A beam of love shall
shine out from your eyes.
A new walk you'll have,
with me by your side.

Marilyn Marinelli

I Saw You

Gentle drips of blood fell from my feet,
shed for you, my child, so that you
would never know defeat.
The storm clouds gathered to pro-
claim this victory over sin,
so you would be strengthened from all your hurts within.
The thorns upon my head were placed
there with great agony,
to bring you peace of mind to set your emotions free.
Free to serve and worship me, to set your spirit free,
from all the turmoil that was placed on
me, on the cross of Calvary.

I saw you bending upon your knees,
with tears streaming from your eyes.
I wanted to cuddle you, as my Father from on high.
But, I had to die to set men free from Satan and his lie.

And as you gently turned with sad-
dened eyes to walk away from me,
my Holy Spirit met you as I hung upon that tree.
To give you hope and peace of mind to set your spirit free,

to let you know I did it all for you,
on the cross of Calvary.

Marilyn Marinelli

Without Wings

I watched you flutter around like a bird without wings,
straining and striving to grasp what life brings.
You wander around like a bird without wings,
not looking and learning of what my word brings.

This sadness of sorrow and life's lonely path,
has kept you bound to the ground as a bird with no wings.
But I have created you from the start,
to have wings to fly my salvation I impart.

Look around! Look around! to the wings that are yours.
Your time to fly was salvation bought.

This sadness of sorrow is dirt hardened fast,
to things of this life, things of the past.
Grime and dirt has covered these wings,
that were meant for you to fly above earthly things.

As I wash off the grime with each passing of time.
Know that your sorrow will ever be mine.

I took all your pain on Calvary's tree.
It was placed there as sin to set you free.

Free from your sorrows and sins open door.
A test of time will be no more.

For all of your tomorrows are gone from your day.
A new walk I will give you as you fly away.
Away from the hurts the sadness of years,
You will soar as an eagle and hold nothing near.

For I have promised you days of "Sunshine" and light.
I'm with you, my child, as you walk thru the night.
I'll wash all the grime of passing time.
You'll have new tomorrows forever be mind.

The laughter that's hidden will shine as light.
All will be better. I'll make things all right.
So don't be discouraged and don't dismay.
A new light I'll give you. A new gentle way.

The bird now will soar for she know who she is.
No more to be bound to the lies that were hid.
Soar! Soar! fly away into the light of a brighter
day. Never more to wander or go astray.

Marilyn Marinelli

My Prayer

Jesus, my love, how can I explain
the misery and doubt, that has plague my mortal plain.
The hurts the fears, the doubt, the tears,
since I walked away that day,
and reached out to do my own thing,
in my weak and shallow way.

The road I walked away from you,
was not a pretty sight.
I cried and cried and pleaded,
"Lord, help me see the light."

I promise I'll not wander,
and promise not to fight.
Lord help me to walk with you,
in your glorious shining light.

I know that I'm not perfect,
and know that I can't be,
the wonderful creation
that you want for me to be.

Unless, I reach for your hand,
and your gentle loving way.
Or, I may find myself a wandering
being forever led astray.

Marilyn Marinelli

Where Are You
My Lord My Savior
My King

I sit beside you watching as you
struggle through your night.

I watch you turn and toss, to the
things that grip your sight.

For all alone I watch you, with a watchful eye,

Feeling the sadness that surrounds your ever turning tide.

The waves have lifted up upon your sadden soul ...

yet you seem to ignore the truth to make you whole.

You struggle in your darkness holding on to your despair.

I told you that I loved you that I
would watch and be there.

But, you have wonder in your darkness
never allowing the light to shine.

So instead of gladness, you have been cov-
ered with this sadness all the time.

Don't watch me when you want me,
watch me because I care.

Don't you know I'm the one that can
get you out of this snare?

What happened to your once upon a time,
with all its hopeful thoughts.
It was stolen from you with lies of different sorts.
So turn away, Turn away, from the gloom of your night.
Sit up my child .... of sadness this day you are reborn.
Don't sit alone and wonder about this lonely silent storm.
Reach out to higher ground where the light does shine.

For I told you, your once upon a
time is where you belong.
Don't run and hide from light that
is shed as a beam for you,
for your tomorrows will be bright and brand new.

Sit at night and rest your head upon your pillow sleep.
And remember, I am with you, my
salvation you can keep.
Look up to heaven, to the brightness of
the sky and remember I am near,
never more to wander in this darkness and fear.

You alone are worthy of my hand at times like this,
for you alone have reached out in search of care and bliss.
Reach out your arms to heaven and seal a fate that soars,
to the highest help from heaven your life to you restored.

Marilyn Marinelli

Animals Are Special

Animals are special
They truly are,
Given from God
To protect and adore.

Some call them children
Dressed in fur coats.
But, I see them ore,
As God's love to adore.

Giving each animal
A special design.
Each could state
"I am of a special kind."

Each has to offer some
Goodness and grace.
All we should take time
To look in their face.

Marilyn Marinelli

Arise And Shine

Father God, as I arise from my slumber,

I stretch my arms out to Thee,

for no other help I know.

This is the day that You have made;

I arise and I am glad in it.

My shower is the cleansing blood of Jesus.

I sit down for breakfast;

I thank Thee, Father, for the fruit of the Spirit,

and that you fill my mouth with good things,

so that my youth is renewed like the eagle's.

Now, Heavenly Father, I go to my prayer closet;

I put on the whole armor of God

that will prepare me for battle.

As I go out of the door, behold!

There stands Goodness and Mercy,

ready to follow me all the days of my life.

Purposeful, I clutch Your agenda,
determined that Thy will be done.
Rejoicing, I sing Your praises,
covered by the shadow of Thy wings.

Marilyn Marinelli

I AM THERE

In the midst of your confusion I am there
to wipe away your every care.
I sit beside you everyday
hoping you'd reach out
so I can show you the way.

In the mist of your confusion I am there
To wash away you're every care.
When trouble seems to surround you
Know my friend that "I AM" is around you.

For trouble may come from every side
Yet, in my love you shall abide.
And every care that seems too hard to do
My grace and love will see you through.

Marilyn Marinelli

Shower Me

Water me Lord with you love.
Shower me with your Words from above.
Fill me Lord with you mercy and grace,
That I may behold your face.
Help me to grow and help me to see,
The wonder you have worked in me.

Marilyn Marinelli

REACH OUT

There is a healing in my heart,
For your soul to have a new start,
Just reach out with your faith
And believe.

For the changes will come
You will start to see them one by one
Just reach out with your faith
And believe.

When my work is done
You will be walking in my Son
Just reach out with your faith
And believe.

Marilyn Marinelli

Turn And Walk Away

Turn away, turn away from the unrealities of life.
Take up a new walk with God with your husband or wife.
For when the walk has slowed you down
And you have no where to go
Go and confess to God
He will surely forgive you so,

Then the road you travel will not be tainted with sin
For you have moved from the deceptions and lies
That have kept you bound by unreal longings within.

Move on to better things as God leads you along
No more to wander on things that are still wrong.
The future will be brighter than snow
As you walk through this life,
Your new walk will glow.

Filled with the promises from our Father above
Filled with joy, innocence and true love.
Restore, restore me my Father God on high
Take away my anger and all of my pride.

Help me to walk a new walk with you,

One that will make me all shiny and new.
Thank you dear Father for your love, mercy and grace.
Thank you for restoring a smile on my face.

Marilyn Marinelli

CANDY

My dog Candy is beautiful
You see.
She is given from God,
From eternity.

She's a blessing of love,
And kindness too.
She's always around,
And wants to know what's new.

She sings in her way,
As most dogs do.
As each day, I sing of the
Glory of God so new.

She is always in prayer,
Each morning with us.
She barks, and barks
And tells God her stuff.

And when our prayers
Are through.
She praises God

As if she knew.

She is my collie
From heaven above
For me to cherish
Adore and love.

Marilyn Marinelli

Seeking God

I sat around each lonely day
Wondering what to do.
Then I heard the Savior say,
I am waiting here for you.

I hear your cry at night
And see you wander through your day.
Yet, you try to figure it out
And never ask me which way?

It's such a simple task to do
Seeking me for what you need.
All you have to do is look to me
And allow my Word to lead.

Then doubt will lift from your heart
And you will know just what to do.
For I have not given you a spirit
That keeps you confused all unglued.

Marilyn Marinelli

www.ingramcontent.com/pod-product-compliance
Lightning Source LLC
Chambersburg PA
CBHW031302060726
47590CB00003B/1021